A Garland of Mantras to aid Spiritual Growth

By

Raikha Bisnauth

Copyright © 2018 Raikha Bisnauth.

All rights reserved.

ISBN   9781092692465

Introduction

Name of this book

Each mantra is like a flower and when several of them are strung(chanted) together, they form a garland; mantras are chanted for several reasons, the principal one being to aid in spiritual growth. Thus, the title of this book **"A Garland of Mantras to promote spiritual growth"** is appropriate.

Reasons for writing this book

I grew up going to mandirs (temples), pujas (religious ceremonies) and satsangas (associations of devotees who seek to rise above the body/mind/intellect complex) where mantras are chanted. To my utter shame though I participated in the chanting, I did not know the meaning the mantras that I chanted. Dare I say that many devotees are in a similar predicament as mine.

This word by word translation of the mantras contained within this book, will not only improve my knowledge but also those of other devotees. This approach will act as a motivation to aid in my spiritual growth and those of other spiritual aspirants.

Historical origins of mantras

Gonda (1963) and Staal (1996) perceived mantras to be older than 1000 B.C. Staal (1996) goes on to add that mantras in Hinduism (Sanatan Dharma) emerged into a combination of art and science in the period 1000 B.C. to 500 B.C.

Reference

Gonda J (1963) - The Indian Mantra - Oriens, Vol 16, page 244-297.

Staal F (1996) - Rituals and Mantras - Motilal Banarsidas, Delhi 110 007, India- Rules without meaning.

What is a Mantra

A mantra is a form of words which when chanted, calms, soothes, protects and purifies the mind, so that it is able to focus on the object of meditation which is pleasing The Lord.

Some perceived benefits of chanting a mantra

i) Physiological

- Increased energy levels.
- More efficient Respiratory system.
- Lower risk of heart disease.
- Immune system is better able to fight infections.
- Academic achievements, decision making, and creativity are improved.
- There is a slowing down of the ageing process.

ii) Psychological

- Promotes self-confidence.
- Strengthens focus and concentration.
- Improves memory.
- Aids peace of mind, calmness and emotional maturity.
- Leads to the development of a strong will power.

iii) Spiritual

- The chanter becomes more compassionate and caring over a period of time.
- The spiritual aspirant (sadhaka) sees the Lord in everyone and everything he or she looks at.

Reference

Bisnauth R (2018) - Hinduism (Sanatan Dharma) - For the Enthusiastic Novice - R. Bisnauth - Page 212-213.

Some occasions when mantras are chanted

Mantras are usually chanted at all the following occasions:
- During pujas or worship in a mandir (temples) and in private homes.
- During religious ceremonies.
- As part of the process of dhyanam (meditation).

Mantras in this book

All the mantras in this book are those that I grew up listening to being chanted; even to this day, these mantras are still popular.

Rules for chanting a Mantra

- **Anugraha** - (the grace of The Lord) - nothing is possible without the grace of The Lord so, before commencement of chanting, the spiritual aspirant (sadhaka) should pray for the Lord's blessing.
- **Guru** - (spiritual master) Initiation - it is the usual practice for a guru to whisper a mantra in the ear of his disciple (shishya) for him or her to chant for life.
- **In the absence of a Guru** - (spiritual master) the spiritual aspirant (sadhaka) can chant a mantra of his or her choice.
- **Hygiene** - It is advisable to have a bath before chanting as it creates a spiritual atmosphere (sattva).
- **Asana** - (seat) - since chanting is time consuming, it is important that the spiritual aspirant (sadhaka) is comfortably seated to minimize distraction during chanting.
- **Environment for chanting** - a quiet, warm, well ventilated environment enhances the effectiveness of the chanting.
- **A Rudraksha or a crystal bead mala** - consisting of 108 beads is recommended for use.
- **A murti in** - the form of an idol or a photo of your expression of The Lord is a very useful source of concentration.

Foreword

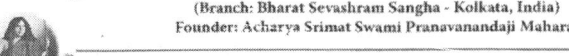

BHARAT SEVASHRAM SANGHA CANADA
(Branch: Bharat Sevashram Sangha - Kolkata, India)
Founder: Acharya Srimat Swami Pranavanandaji Maharaj

December 23, 2018

FOREWORD

In this book which translates the literal, verbatim rendition of the popular mantras which millions of Hindu devotees learn by rote and fervently repeat at mandirs and pujas, Pandit Raikha Bisnauth Tiwari continues his magnanimous efforts to project our age-old Hindu religion in ways that would make it more meaningful, especially for the younger generation of Hindus who do not understand Hindi but nevertheless repeat the mantras with fervor; I sincerely believe that this book will enrich all Hindus and further facilitate their achievement of heavenly bliss.

This is obviously a great labour of love from which all readers will benefit tremendously.

While I cannot add to the content and quality of the book, I take this opportunity to encourage all Hindus to use it to enrich their prayers and enhance their devotion to the Lord.

Swami Bhajanananda - Adhyaksha
Bharat Sevashram Sangha Canada.
Hindu Heritage Inc.

---

102 Rivalda Road, Toronto, Ontario M9M 2M8 Tel: (416) 741-4335 • Fax: (416) 744-6305

HEAD OFFICE: Bharat Sevashram Sangha, 211 Rash Behari Avenue, Kolkata - 19, India
BRANCHES: Delhi, Brindavan, Kurukshetra, Gujarat - Ahmedabad, Surat, Dwarka, Mumbai, Haridwar, Varanasi, Badrinath, Kedarnath, Rameshwaram, Kanyakumari, Ghatsila, Jamshedpur, Jammu, etc. OVERSEAS: London, U.S.A., Canada, Trinidad, Guyana, Fiji, etc.

Dedications

I am indebted to Sri Ganesh (who is The Lord of the world) for gracing me with the opportunity to write this book.

I am also indebted to the following embodiments of the Atma (Soul) for their contributions in making this book into reality; these are:

i) **My Parents**

My parents Pandit Bisnauth Tiwari and Sumintra Bisnauth Tiwari who fed me on a diet of spiritual pursuits throughout my formative years.

ii) **Pandit Pitamber Dindayal**

Pandit Ji was instrumental in motivating me to walk on the spiritual path, by being a positive role model in our weekly meetings at his home.

iii) **My wife Tarawattee Devi**

My wife who is a dedicated practitioner of karma yoga (the discipline of action) and bhakti yoga (the discipline of devotion), added to my thirst to want to walk the spiritual path.

iv) **Sri Krishna Bhardwaj and Kanta Bhardwaj**

Sri Krishna Ji and Kanta Ji not only hosted me but made it possible for me to go on pilgrimage, sampled life in ashrams, attended satsangas and purchased some our major religious books.

v) **Sri Virender Sharma and Uma Sharma**

I was introduced to Sri Virender and Uma Sharma by Kanta Ji (Uma Ji and Kanta Ji are sisters). I refer to Virender Ji as my Atma Bhai as I felt from the moment we met, as if we had known each other in many past lives. They were very gracious in not only hosting me but took it upon themselves to make sure that each trip to India was positively maximized in a spiritual sense.

Acknowledgments

I very thankfully acknowledge the contributions of the following individuals in the preparation of this book:

Vijay Vishnu Bisnauth

Vijay has been very instrumental in aiding in the organization of this entire Lord's manuscript, to make it user friendly for established devotees both young and old.
He has used his skills of innovation to set out the mantras in a manner that makes it appealing to all devotees.

Acharya Bankim Gossai M.B.E.

Atma Bhai Bankim Gossai not only proof read the Lord's manuscript but has made very valuable suggestions for its improvements; some changes have been made to reflect his thinking.

Devendra Ramdehal

The design of the front and back covers including the photograph, are the brain child of Devindra; he has drawn on his experience of working in the field of marketing, publishing and as a practitioner of Hinduism (Sanatan Dharma) in the USA, to design this masterpiece.

CONTENTS

	Introduction	i
	Foreword	vi
	Dedications	vii
	Acknowledgments	Ix
1	Om (Aum - The Lord) Namaskar (Salutations)	Pg 1
2	Sri Ganesh Ji (The Lord) Namaskar (Salutations)	Pg 7
3	Maha Lakshmi Mata (Mother) Namaskar (Salutations)	Pg 25
4	Mata (Mother) Saraswati Namaskar (salutations)	Pg 37
5	Bhagavan (The Lord) Vishnu Namaskar (Salutations)	Pg 47
6	Bhagavan (The Lord) Sri Rama Namaskar (Salutations)	Pg 61
7	Sri Hanuman Ji Namaskar (Salutations)	Pg 71
8	Bhagavan (The Lord) Sri Krishna Namaskar (Salutations)	Pg 80
9	Bhagavan (The Lord) Shiva Namaskar (Salutations)	Pg 90
10	Sri Durga Mata (Mother) Namaskar (Salutations)	Pg 103
11	Surya Devata Namaskar (Salutation)	Pg 115
12	Shanti (Peace) Namaskar (Salutations)	Pg 125

1 Om (Aum - The Lord) Namaskar (Salutations)

Definition of Om (Aum)

Om (Aum) is The Lord without form (Nirguna Brahman) and the lord with form (Saguna Brahman e.g. Ganesh, Vishnu, Rama, and Krishna). Om (Aum) is that which pervades life and the breath or prana (Pranava). It is the source of all mantras (**man**-mind, **tra**-a tool for freeing).

Reference

Lochtefeld J (2002) - Pranava -The Illustrated Encylopaedia of Hinduism - NZ Publishing - Vol 2, P522.

Om is Pronounced

Aum

Om (Aum - The Lord) is The Highest Goal

Kathopanisad 1:11:15 presents Om (Aum) as the highest goal thus:

*Sarve vedaa yat padam amananti,
*tapaamsi sarvani ca yat vadanti;
*yad icchanto brahma-caryam caranti,
*tat te padam sangrahena bravimy-om-ity-etat.

Word by word translation of this mantra

**Sarve* - all; *vedaa* - vedaas; *yat* - that; *padam* - goal; *amananti* - praise,

ptapaamsi - acts of austerities; *sarvani* - all; *ca* - and; *yad* - which; *vadanti* - declare,

pyad - which; *icchanto* - desiring; *brahma-caryam* - practice of self-discipline; *caranti* - lead,

tat - that; *te* - your; *padam* - goal; *sangrahena* - briefly; *braveemy* - I will tell you,

Om (Aum) -The Lord; *ity* - that; *etat* - it is.

General translation of this mantra

That goal which the vedas praise as the highest, which is revealed by austerities only and which is earned by those, who practice self-control, I will tell you-**It is Om (Aum).**

Origins of Om (Aum)

Om (Aum) is the primordial sound or cosmic sound or mystical sound. Before creation of the universe took place, it is believed that there was only a natural humming sound which mirrors the sound of Om (Aum). This sound of Om (Aum) was instrumental in the manifestation of our creation.

Reference

Swami Chinmayananda (2000) – Kathopanisad - A dialogue with death - CCMT, Mumbai, 400 072, India - 1:11:15.

Swami Lokeswarananda (2009) - Katha Upanisad - Ramakrishna Mission Institute of Culture, Kolkata, 700 029, India - 1:11:15.

Why all rituals commence and end with the chanting of Om (Aum)

Om (Aum) is the most sacred syllable and symbol of The Lord; it is referred to as the **Pranava Mantra (that which pervades life and runs through Prana or breath).** As a result of it being the name and symbol of The Lord it is chanted:

- **At the beginning** of all religious ceremonies, to seek the grace of The Lord to invoke His blessings, so that they get off to an auspicious start.
- **During** the religious ceremonies to ensure that they are conducted in the prescribed manner.
- **At the end** of the ceremonies as a thank you to The Lord for a successful outcome.

Reference

Swami Tattvavidananda Saraswati (2004) - Ganapati Upanisad - D.K. Printworld (P) Ltd, New Delhi 110 005, India - P11-13.

Verbal chanting of Om (Aum)

The conditions for chanting Om (Aum) are as follows:
- **Time of the day**-ideally, this should be done at sunrise, noon and sunset.
- **Environment for chanting**-warm, well ventilated, peaceful and comfortable to aid concentration.
- **Seat**-should be comfortable to promote stable support.
- **Seating position**-the lotus position is advisable but, one that is comfortable to the spiritual aspirant (sadhaka) is acceptable.
- **Eyes closed**-during chanting is advisable in order to reduce sensory distraction (s).

The process of verbal chanting of Om (Aum)

- **Breathe in for a count of 8** and with each breath of inspiration, chant Om (Aum).
- **Hold your breath for a mental count of 5**, with each mental count chant Om (Aum).
- **Breathe out for a count of 8** and as you breathe out, chant Om (Aum)
- **Pause for a count of 10**
- **Now repeat the process as stated above.**
- **You can use your fingers** to aid the counting process **or a mala.**

The process of mental chanting of Om (Aum)

- **Follow the same process as in verbal chanting** the only difference is, you are now chanting mentally.

How much time should I devote to the chanting of Om (Aum)

- For the first week, spend one minute per day chanting Om (Aum).
- Then increase the time factor by one minute each day for the second and week.
- Over the next fifteen weeks you would be able to chant for fifteen minutes.

Benefits of chanting Om (Aum)

Psychological
- Over a period of time the spiritual aspirant (sadhaka) becomes peaceful and calm.
- He or she radiates confidence.
- Gains mastery over the mind and the senses.

Physiological
- There are improvements in the health of the individual over a period of time.
- The individual acquires the ability to heal himself or herself and others.

Social
- The presence of the spiritual aspirant (sadhaka) in a social setting, proves beneficial to all those within his or her proximity.

Spiritual
- Radiates love, compassion and empathy.
- Sees the same **Self/Soul (Atma)** in all members of God's creation.

2 Sri Ganesh Ji (The Lord) Namaskar (Salutations)

Some pertinent information about Sri Ganesh are:

i) The name Ganesh

The name Ganesh is a Sanskrit word composed of:
- **Gana** - Lord of created categories.
- **Isha** - Lord or master.

ii) Why Sri Ganesh Ji is worshipped first

- **He appeared** before creation.
  - Ganapati Upanisad P 47-48.
- **Ganapati Upanisad verse 6** informs us that He is Brahma, Vishnu and Mahesh.

The Mantra

Tvam Brahma, tvam Vishnu, tvam Rudra.

Word by word translation of the above verse

Tvam-you; *Brahma*- Brahma the creator; *tvam*-you; *Vishnu*-The protector; *tvam*-you *Rudra*-the annihilator.

General translation of the above verse

Brahma the creator of this world, Vishnu the protector and Rudra the annihilator are expressions of yours.

Reference

Swami Tattvavidananda Saraswati (2004) - Ganapati Upanisad - D.K. Print World (P) Ltd, New Delhi 100 005, India - Verse 6.

iii) Sri Ganesh Ji and Om (Aum)

Sri Ganesh is identified with Om (Aum) because it is His form (Omkar svaroop),.It is the fundamental sound of the universe.

Reference

Swami Tattvavidananda Saraswati (2004) - Ganapati Upanisad - D.K. Print World, New Delhi 110 005, India - Verse 7, P 69.

iv) Sri Ganesh Ji is widely revered as

- Remover of obstacles.
- Patron of the arts.
- Lord of new beginnings.

v) Sri Ganesh Ji is the embodiment of the following virtues

- Buddhi or wisdom.
- Siddhi or attainment/spiritual growth.
- Riddhi or prosperity.

vi) He is associated with

- Saraswati or Sharada (the expression of The Lord who deals with culture and arts).
- Lakshmi (The expression of The Lord associated with material prosperity and spiritual illumination).

vii) His blessings are sought to gain

- A successful marriage.
- To have healthy and intelligent off springs.
- Success in education and employment.
- Food, security, shelter and clothing and good health.
- A positive outcome in religious ceremonies.

Some Popular Mantras of Sri Ganesh Ji

i) Om (Aum) Shukla Ambara Dharam Vishnum

The Mantra

*Om (Aum) Shukla ambara dharam Vishnum,
*Shashi varnam chatur bhujam;
*prasanna vadanam dhyaayet,
*sarva vighno upashantaye.

Word by word translation of this mantra

*Om (Aum) - The foremost name and symbol of The Lord; *Shukla* – white; *ambara* – clothe; *dharam* – wear; *Vishnum* - The all-pervasive Lord,

*Shashi – moon; *varnam* - white colour; *chatur* – four; *bhujam* - hands;

*prasanna - smiling; *vadanam* – face; *dhyaayet* - meditate on,

*sarva – all; *vighno* – obstacles; *upashantaye* - removal of.

General translation of this mantra

We meditate on the all-pervasive Lord, whose name and symbol is Om (Aum), who is clad in white garments, who shines brilliantly as the moon, who has four hands and a smiling face for the removal of the three fold obstacles in our lives. These obstacles are:

- **Adidaivika** - harm emanating from the sky e.g. thunder, lightning, flooding and earthquake etc.
- **Adhibhautica** - harm emanating from this world in the form of murder and theft perpetrated against the devotee etc.
- **Adhyatmica** - problems emanating from within one's self e.g. self-harm, anxiety and depression.

Benefits of chanting this mantra

- Its chanting when done with faith, removes the above-mentioned obstacles.

Reference

Swami Dayananda Saraswati (2005) - Prayer Guide - Arsha Vidya Gurukulum, P.O. Box 1059, Pennsylvania, P.A. 18353, USA - Mantras and Stotras Page 117-119.

ii) **Om Bhadram Karnebhih**

The Mantra

**Om Bhadram karnebhih srunuyam deva,*
*bhadram pashyem akshabhir yajatrah;
*sthirair angais tushtu vaamsah tanu bhih,
*vyashema deva hitam yadaayuh;
*svasti na indro vrddashravah,
*svasti na poosha vishva deva;
*svasti na staarksyo aristanemih,
*svasti no brhaspatir dadhaatu;
*Om shanti,
*Om shanti,
*Om shanti.

Word by word translation of this mantra

Om (Aum) - the foremost name and symbol of The Lord; *Bhadram* - The auspicious; *karnebhih* - with ears; *srunuyam* - may we listen; *deva* - O Gods,

Bhadram - The auspicious; *pashyema* - may we see; *akshabhir* - with our eyes; *yajatrah* - engaged in worship;

Sthirair - strong; *angais* - with limbs; *tushtu vaamsah* - prayerful; *tanu bhih* - with our bodies,

Vyashema - live praising; *deva* - gods; *hita* - given by; *yadaayuh* - given life span;

svasti - well-being; *na*-us; *indro* - Lord Indra;

vrddashravah - of great fame,

*svasti - well-being; *na*-us; *poosha* - Lord surya; *vishva* - universe; *veda* - knower;

*svasti - well-being; *na* - us; *staarksyo* - Garuda; *aristanemih* - the destroyer of adversities,

*svasti - well-being; *na* - us; *brhaspatir* - guru of the demigods; *dadhaatu* - preserve us;

*Om (Aum) - the foremost name and symbol of The Lord; *shanti* - protect us from all harm emanating from divine sources e.g. thunder and lightning (**Adhidaivica**);

*Om (Aum)-the foremost name and symbol of The Lord. *shanti*-protect us from all harm emanating from this earth e.g. murder and theft perpetrated against the devotee (**Adhibhautica**),

*Om (Aum)-the foremost name and symbol of The Lord. *shanti*-protect us from self -harm e.g. self-injury, anxiety and depression (**Adhyatmica**).

General translation of this mantra

O gods, may we always hear what is auspicious, may we always see what is auspicious. May each part of these on loan bodies be healthy and strong so that, we can maximize this life span to satisfy you my Lord.

May we be inspired by Lord Indra to perform auspicious actions. May the omniscient Poosan grace us with the things in life to enable us to carry out our activities of living.

May Garuda (the vehicle of Lord Vishnu) destroy our adversities and grace us with a life that is auspicious. May Lord Brhaspatir grace our lives with glory and preserve us.

May Om (Aum) shanti - protect us from all harm emanating from divine sources e.g. thunder and lightning (**Adhidaivica**).

May Om (Aum) shanti - protect us from all harm emanating from this earth e.g. murder, theft, disease and defects (**Adhibhautica**).

May Om (Aum) shanti - protect us from all forms of self-harm e.g. self-injury and anxiety (**Adhyatmica**).

Benefits of chanting this mantra

- The spiritual aspirant (sadhaka) is blessed with an auspicious life.

Reference

Swami Lokeswarananda - (2011) - Prashna Upanisad-Ramakrishna Mission Institute of Culture, Kolkata 700 029, India - Invocation.

Swami Tattvavidananda Saraswati (2004) - Ganapati Upanisad-D.K. Print World (P) Ltd, New Delhi,110 015, India - P 11-12.

iii) Om (Aum)Vakra tunda mahakaya

The Mantra

Om (Aum) Vakra tunda Mahakaya,
Surya koti sama prabha;
nirvighnam kuru me deva,
sarva karyeshu sarvada.

Word by word translation of this mantra

Om (Aum) - the foremost name and symbol of The Lord; *vakra tunda* - curved trunk; *maha* - large; *kaya* - body,

Surya - sun; *koti* - millions of; *sama* - equal; *prabha* – splendour;

nirvighnam - free of all obstacles; *kuru* - make me; *deva* - O Lord,

sarva- always; *karyeshu*-work or activities; *sarvada*-forever.

General translation of this mantra

O Divine Lord Ganesh with a curve trunk and a large body, the one whose splendour equals a million sun, please grace this existence with freedom from all obstacles e.g. psychological, physical, social and spiritual so that, my spiritual growth can be assured.

Benefits of chanting this mantra

- It destroys all obstacles in the path of the spiritual aspirant (sadhaka).
- It aids spiritual growth.

Reference

Jagannathan S and Krishna M (1992) - Ganesh, The auspicious. The Beginning-Vakils, Feffer and Simpson Ltd, Bombay, 400 038, India - P5.

iv) Om (Aum) Gam Ganpataye Namaha

The Mantra

*Om (Aum) Gam Ganapatye namaha

Word by word translation of this mantra

**Om* (Aum) - the foremost name and symbol of The Lord; *Gam* - my prostration unto Lord Ganesh; *gana* - groups; *pataye* - Lord of; *namah* - my salutation and surrender.

General translation

I offer my sincerest salutation and surrender to The Lord of the world.

Benefits of chanting this mantra

When chanted this mantra, this mantra confers success before the commencement of:
- Journeys.
- Education.
- Employment.
- Business.

Reference

Swami Tattvavidananda Saraswati (2004)- Ganapati Upanisad-D.K. Print World (P) Ltd, Bali Nagar, New Delhi, 100 015, India- Pages 24, 69, 71 and 72.

v) Twelve (12) Word Mantras in praise of Sri Ganesh Ji

The Mantras

*Om (Aum) vakratundaya namah.
*Om (Aum) eka danta namah.
*Om (Aum) Krishna ping akscha namah.
*Om (Aum) gaje vaktram namah.
*Om (Aum) lambodaram namah.
*Om (Aum) vikat namah.
*Om (Aum) vighna raja namah.
*Om (Aum) dhoomra varnam namah.
*Om (Aum) bhala chandram namah.
*Om (Aum) vinayakam namah.
*Om (Aum) ganapatim namah.
*Om (Aum) gajananam namah.

Word by word translation of this mantra

*Om (Aum) - the foremost name and symbol of The Lord; *vakratundaya* - The Lord with a curved trunk; *namah* - I offer my salutation and surrender.

*Om (Aum) - The Lord; *Eka-danta* - The lord with one tusk; *namah* - my salutation and surrender.

* Om (Aum) - The Lord; *Krishna ping akscha* - The Lord with dark brown eyes; *namah* - my salutation and surrender.

*Om (Aum) - The Lord; *Gajavaktram* - The Lord with an elephant face; *namah* - my salutation and surrender.

*Om (Aum) - The Lord; *Lambodaram* - The Lord with a large abdomen; namah - my salutation and surrender.

* *Om* (Aum) - The Lord; *Vikat* - The Lord with a huge body; *namah* - my salutation and surrender.

* *Om* (Aum) - The Lord; *Vighna rajam* - The Lord who removes obstacles; *namah* - my salutation and surrender.

* *Om* (Aum) - The Lord; *Dhoomra varna* - The Lord who is dark in colour; *namah* - my salutation and surrender.

* *Om* (Aum) - The Lord; *Bhalachandram* - The Lord whose face is adorned by the moon; *namah* - my salutation and surrender.

* *Om* (Aum) - The Lord; *Vinayakam* - The Lord who removes all obstacles; *namah* - my salutation and surrender.

* *Om* (Aum) - The Lord; *Ganapatim* - Lord of the celestial attendants; *namah* - my salutation and surrender;

* *Om* (Aum) - The Lord; *Gajananam* - The lord with an elephant (gaja) face (ananam); *namah* - my salutation and surrender.

General translation of this mantra

O Lord Ganesh with a curved trunk, one tusk, dark brown eyes, elephant face, large abdomen, huge body, dark in colour, whose face is adorned with the moon, Lord of celestial attendants, remover of obstacles, I pray that you grace this existence with freedom from all obstacles so that my journey throughout this life is successful.

Benefits of chanting this Mantra

- It aids the chanter in being successful in all his or her endeavours.

Reference

Chaturvedi B.K. (1996) - Ganesh (Gods and Goddesses of India:1) - Books for All-Delhi 110 052, India - Pages 11 and 41.

vi) Om (Aum) Gajananam bhuta ganadi sevitam

The Mantra

> *Om Gajananam bhuta ganadi sevitam,*
> *kapitha jambu phalasaara bhaksitam;*
> *Uma sutam shoka vinasha karanam,*
> *namami vighneswara pada pankajam.*

Word by word translation of this mantra

**Om (Aum)* - The foremost name and symbol of The Lord. *gajananam* - elephant faced Lord; *bhuta* - celestials; *ganadi* - group; *sevitam* - served by,

**kapitha* - wood apple; *jambu* - rose apple; *phala* - fruit; *saara* - essence; *bhaksitam* - eater;

**Uma* - The Goddess Parvati; *sutam* - son of ;*shoka* - suffering; *vinasha* - destruction; *karanam* - reason or cause;

**namami* - I prostrate; *vighneshwara* - The remover of obstacles; *pada* - feet; *pankajam* - lotus.

General translation of this mantra

O elephant faced Lord who is served by celestial attendants, who dines on His favourite wood and rose apple fruits, who is the son of mother Parvati, the destroyer of sufferings; I prostrate myself at your lotus feet beseeching you, to destroy all obstacles to my spiritual progress.

Benefits of chanting this mantra

It aids the promotion of spiritual growth.

Reference

Jagannathan S and Krishna N (1992) - Ganesh (The auspicious   The Beginning) - Vakils, Feffer and Simon Ltd, Bombay 400 038, India - Page 14.

vii) Sri Ganesh Ji's Gayatri Mantra

The Mantra

*Om eka dantaya vidmahe,
*vakra tundaya dheemahi,
*tanno danti prachodayat.

Word by word translation of this mantra

Om (Aum) - the foremost name and symbol of The Lord; *eka* - one; *dantaya* - tusk; *vidmahe*-we devote our selves to the omnipresent Lord,

vakra tundaya - The lord with the curved trunk; *dheemahi* - we meditate on Him;

tanno - guide us; *danti* - may the one tusk one; *prachodayat* - direct, inspire and enlighten our minds with wisdom.

General translation

We pray to the omnipresent Lord with a single tusk and a curved trunk, to bless us with an intellect in the mode of goodness (sattva). We prostrate ourselves at your lotus feet with the request that you enhance our spiritual growth so that we can realize, that we are the soul (Atma) and not this body/mind/intellect complex (anatma).

Benefits of chanting this mantra

- It enhances spiritual growth.

Reference

Swami Tattvavidananda Saraswati (2004)-Ganapati Upanisad-D.K. Print World (P) Ltd, Delhi 110 015, India-Verse11, Page 11.

3 Maha Lakshmi Mata (Mother) Namaskar (Salutations)

Who is Lakshmi?

Lakshmi is the expression of The Lord, who is responsible for the provision of resources for the maintenance of the universe. She is also the source of spiritual illumination.

Origin of the word Lakshmi

Lakshmi comes from the Sanskrit word **Laksme** meaning **aim** or **goal.**

Lakshmi is referred to as Sri

Lakshmi, the expression of The Lord who is responsible, for resource provision for the maintenance of the universe as well as the source of spiritual illumination, is referred to as **Sri,** because she is endowed with six auspicious qualities. These qualities are;
- Vairagya - absolute detachment.
- Jnana - absolute knowledge.
- Virya - absolute strength.
- Yashas - absolute fame.
- Sri - absolute wealth.
- Aishwarya - absolute over lordship.

Reference

Swami Dayananda Saraswati (2006) - Bhagavad Gita (Home Study Course) - Arsha Vidya Gurukulum, Coimbatore 641 108, India-Vol 3, Page 515.

Some popular Maha Lakshmi Mata Mantra

i) Mahalakshmi Stotram (A Hymn of praise)

The Stotram

>*Om (Aum) padma asana stithe devi,
>*Para Brahma svaroopini;
>*Paramesi jagan mata,
>*Maha Lakshmi namosthute.

Word by word translation of this Stotram

Om (Aum) - the foremost name and symbol of The Lord; *padma* - lotus; *asana* - seat; *stithe* - who has; *devi* - mother Goddess,

Para - infinite or ultimate; *Brahma* - Lord; *svaroopini* - essential nature;

Paramesi - The Lord; *jagan* - the world; *mata* - mother,

Maha - great; *Lakshmi* - the expression of The Lord responsible for resource provision, for the maintenance of the universe as well as spiritual illumination; *namo* - I offer my salutations and surrender; *sthute* - unto you.

General translation of this Stotram

I offer my sincerest salutation and surrender to Divine Mother Lakshmi, who is seated on a Lotus flower (the symbol of purity and auspiciousness), who is the universal Mother, whose essential nature is Absolute Existence (Sat), Absolute Consciousness (Cit) and Absolute Bliss (Ananda) and who is the goal of Life.

Benefits of chanting this mantra

- This mantra confers material and spiritual growth.

Reference

Original source unknown.

ii) Om (Aum) Sarvaagne Sarva Varade

The Mantra

Om (Aum) sarva agne sarva varade,
sarva dushta bhayamkari;
sarva duhkha hare devi,
Maha Lakshmi namosthute

Word by word translation of this mantra

Om (Aum) - the foremost name and symbol of The Lord; *sarva agne* - knower of everything; *sarva* - all; *varade* - bestower of,

sarva - all; *dushta* - wickedness or immorality; *bhayamkari* - fearless;

sarva - all; *duhkha* - misery or frustration; *hare* - one who takes away grief or suffering; *devi* - divine goddess,

Maha - great; *Lakshmi* - mother of material and spiritual wealth and the goal of life; *namo* - I offer my salutation and surrender; *sthute* - unto you.

General translation of this mantra

I offer my sincerest salutation and surrender to The Divine Mother Lakshmi who is an expression of The Lord, the knower of everything, the bestower of all our needs, the remover our miseries, sufferings and the destroyer of the wicked.

Benefits of chanting this mantra

- This mantra will destroy our internal and external enemies.

Reference

Original source unknown.

iii) Shubham karoti kalyanam

The Mantra

*Om (Aum) shubham karoti kalyanam,
*arogyam dhana sampadah;
*shatru buddhi vinashaya,
*deepa jyotir namosthute.

Word by word translation of this mantra

Om (Aum) - The Lord; *shubham* - auspiciousness; *karoti* - which brings; *kalyanam* - progress and prosperity,

arogyam - freedom from ill health; *dhana* - wealth; *sampadah* - bountiful;

shatru - ignorance; *buddhi* - intellect; *vinashaya* - destruction,

deepa - lamp; *jyotir* - of light; *namo* - my salutation and surrender; *sthute* - unto you.

General translation

I offer my sincerest salutation and surrender, to The Divine Mother Lakshmi, who is the lamp light of spiritual and material progress, good health and the remover of ignorance which is a barrier to our spiritual growth.

Benefits of chanting this mantra

- This mantra destroys the intellect's enemy which is ignorance which is a barrier to our spiritual growth.
- This mantra is chanted when the diya or lamp is lit.

Reference

Original source unknown.

vi) Deepo Jyotir Para Brahma

The Mantra

Deepo Jyotir Para Brahma,
deepo jyotir Janardana;
deepo hara tu me papam,
sandhya deepam namosthute.

Word by word translation of this mantra

* *Deepo* - lamp; *jyotir* - light; *Para* - infinite; *Brahma* - The Lord.

deepo - lamp; *jyoti*r - light; *Janardana* - a name of Lord Krishna;

deepo - lamp; *hara* - destroyer; *tu* - whereas; *me* - my; *papam* - sins,

sandhya - dawn and dusk; *deepam* - light; *namo* - salutation and surrender; *sthute* - unto you.

General translation of this mantra

I offer my sincerest salutation and surrender to the infinite Lord, whose presence is light; I pray that She destroy my sins and ignorance which are barriers to my spiritual growth.

Benefits of chanting this mantra

- It aids spiritual growth

Reference

Original source unknown.

vii) Karagre vasate Lakshmi

The Mantra

Om (Aum) Karagre vasate Lakshmi,
kara madhye Saraswati;
kara mule tu Govinda,
prabhate kara darshanam.

Word by word translation of this mantra

Om (Aum) - The foremost name and symbol of The Lord; *karagre* - on my fingers; *vasate* - dwells; *Lakshmi* - the expression of The Lord who provide resources and liberation from birth and death,

kara - on the palms of my hands; *madhye* - middle; *Saraswati* - the expression of The Lord who is the source of all knowledge and the essence of the self;

kara - hands; *mule* – base; *tu* - whereas; *Govinda* - The Lord who pervades and energizes all the worlds,

prabhate - in the morning; *kara* - hands; *darshanam* - look at.

General translation of this mantra

I offer my sincerest salutation and surrender to The Lord of the world, for residing on the tips of my fingers in His expression as mother Lakshmi, On the middle of my palms in His expression as mother Saraswati, and on the base of my hands in His original form as Govinda.

Benefits of chanting this mantra

- This mantra seeks the blessings of the Lord to ensure that each performed action are done for the welfare of all God's creation.

Reference

Original source unknown.

4 Maa (Mother) Saraswati Namaskar (salutations)

Definition of Saraswati

- **Saras** - essence
- **Swa** - The Self
- **Saraswati** - the essence of The Self

Maa Saraswati is referred to as:

The expression of The Lord responsible for education and wisdom which are needed for creation to take place.

Maa Saraswati is the patron of:

- Education.
- Music.
- Arts.
- Speech.

Maa Saraswati is:

- The Mother of the Vedas

Some Popular Maa (mother) Saraswati Mantras

i) Yaa Kunden Du Tusaara Haar Dhavala

The Mantra

*Om (Aum) Yaa kunden du tusaar haar dhavalaa,
*yaa shubra vastra aavrataa;
*yaa veena var danda manditta karaa,
yaa shveta padma asana;
*yaa Brahma Achyuta Shankar prabhrtibhih,
*Devaih sadaa poojita;
*saa mam paatu Saraswati Bhagavati,
*nishshesa jaa dhyaapaha.

Word by word translation of this mantra

*Om (Aum) - the foremost name and symbol of The Lord; *yaa* - she; *kunden* - a jasmine flower; *du* - the moon; *tusaar* - of snowflakes; *haar* - a garland; *dhavalaa* - dazzling white,

*yaa - she; *shubra* - white; *vastra* - clothes or garments; *aavrataa* - wears;

*yaa - she; *veena* - stringed musical instrument; *vara* - boon; *danda* - staff; *manditta* - are adorned; *karaa* - whose hands,

*yaa - she; *shveta* - white; *padma* - lotus; *asana* - seated;

*yaa - she; *Brahma* - The expression of The Lord

as the creator; *Achyuta* - Krishna an expression of The Lord; *Shankar* - an expression of The Lord as the reabsorber of universe; *prabhrtibhih* - from the beginning;

*devaih - demigods; *sada* - always; *poojita* - worshipped;

*saa - she; *mam* - me; *paatu* - protect; *Saraswati* - Mother Saraswati; *Bhagavati* - Divine Mother;

*nishshesa - endless; *jaadhdhya* - ignorance; *apahaa* - remove.

General translation

I offer my sincerest salutation and surrender to mother Saraswati Bhagavati (The expression of The Lord who deals with knowledge and wisdom), who is clothed in white garments, is garlanded by snow white lilies, in whose hands are a veena and a giving staff, who is seated on a white lotus, who is worshipped by the expressions of The Lord as the creator, the protector and The reabsorber, I seek your grace not only to remove my endless ignorance but to wrap me in your protective embrace.

Benefits of chanting this mantra

- It provides us with protection against our internal and external enemies.
- It removes the ignorance of forgetfulness of our real nature i.e. we are Atma or the Soul.

Reference
Swami Dayananda Saraswati (2005) - Prayer Guide - Arsha Vidya Gurukulum, P.O. Box 1059, Pennsylvania 18353, USA - Pages 123-127.

ii) **Om (Aum) Saraswati Namastubhyam**

The Mantra

>*Om (Aum) Saraswati namastubhyam,*
>*varade kaama roopini;*
>*vidya arambham karishyami,*
>*siddhir bhavatu me sadaa.*

Word by word translation of this mantra

Om (Aum) - the foremost name and symbol of The Lord; *Saraswati* - the essence of The Self or soul and the expression of The Lord who is the post holder of education and wisdom; *namastubhyam* - my salutations to you,

varade - giver of boons; *kaama* - desire; *roopini* - form or manifestation;

vidya - education; *arambham* - beginning; *karishyami* - doing or performing,

siddhir – accomplishment; *bhavatu* - let it be; *me* - for me; *sadaa* - always.

General translation of this mantra

I offer my sincerest salutation to The lord of the world, who in the form of mother Saraswati is the bestower of education, intelligence and wish fulfillments. As I commence this module of education grace me with success in this undertaking.

Benefits of chanting this mantra

This mantra blesses the student with success in his or her academic pursuit.

Reference

Original source unknown.

iii) **Om (Aum) Shreem**

This mantra

Om (Aum) shreem,
hreem,
Saraswatyai namah

Word by word translation of this mantra

Om (Aum) - the foremost name and symbol of The Lord. *shreem*-material,

hreem - desire for power,

Saraswtyai - the expression of The Lord responsible for education and wisdom; *namah* - I offer my salutations and surrender.

General translation of this mantra

I offer my salutations and surrender to the lotus feet of the expression of The Lord in the form of Mother Saraswati, who manages education and intellect to make Me powerful in this material world.

Benefits of chanting this mantra

- It graces the chanter with influence over others

Reference

Original source unknown.

iv) Om (Aum) Mata Saraswati Sharada

The Mantra

Om (Aum) Mata Saraswati Sharada,
vidya daani dayanti duhkh harini,
jagat janani jvala mukhi,
sudrishti sevak vardan,
taan taal aur aalaap buddhi alankar.

Word by word translation of this mantra

Om (Aum) - the foremost name and symbol of The Lord; *Mata* - Divine Mother; *Saraswati* - The expression of The Lord which is responsible for education and music; *Sharada* - name for Mother Saraswati,

vidya - knowledge; *daani* - giver of; *dayanti* - Lord of compassion; *duhkh* - sorrow; *harini* - remover of,

jagat - world; *janani* - Mother of; *jvala* - fire; *mukhi* - mouth;

sudrishti - auspicious attention; *sevak* - servant; *vardan* - boon;

taan - musical work; *taal* - rhythm; *aalaap* - commencement; *buddhi* - knowledge; *alankar* - jewel.

General translation of this mantra

Dear Divine mother Saraswati, you are The Lord of compassion, knowledge and the eradicator of distress; You are my mother, the fire mouthed one. I your humble servant pray that you bless us, with auspiciousness, musical mastery and knowledge.

Benefits of this mantra

- This mantra will grace musicians with a knowledgeable and soothing voice.

Reference

Original source unknown.

v) Om (Aum) Aim Saraswatyai Namah

The mantra

*Om (Aum) aim Saraswatyai namah

Word by word translation of this mantra

Om (Aum) - The foremost name and symbol of The Lord; aim - beej or seed mantra; Saraswatya - The expression of The Lord responsible for knowledge and wisdom and who, is the essence of The Self; namah - my salutation and surrender.

General translation of this mantra

I offer my sincerest salutation and surrender to The Lord, who is the expression of knowledge, wisdom and who is the essence of The Self Aatma.

Benefits of chanting this mantra

This mantra will be useful to those who are ideas generators.

Reference

Original source unknown.

5 Bhagavan (The Lord) Vishnu Namaskar (Salutations)

Who is Bhagavan Vishnu?

Vishnu is the principal deity of Hinduism (Sanatan Dharma). He is the maintainer and protector of all members of creation. He is also the deity of peace.

What is the meaning of Bhagavan?

One who has the six-fold virtues in absolute measure (**Bhaga**). The six-fold virtues are:
- **Jnana** (absolute knowledge).
- **Vairagya** (absolute detachment).
- **Virya** (absolute capacity to create, maintain and resolve).
- **Yashas** (absolute fame).
- **Sri** (absolute wealth).
- **Aishwarya** (absolute over lordship).

Role of Bhagavan Vishnu

His portfolio of responsibilities includes:
- Maintainer of order.
- Promoter of Dharma (virtuous conduct).
- Establishment of Satya the religion of truth.
- Loving all members of His creation.
- Promoter and maintainer of peace.

Avatars of Bhagavan Vishnu

When the above-mentioned roles are compromised or threatened, He descends into the material world to re-establish these values. His avatars (descent into the material world) thus far are;
- Matsya - Fish.
- Kurma - Tortoise.
- Varaha - Boar.
- Vamana - The dwarf.
- Narasimha - Half man half lion.
- Parasurama - Fierce warrior who rid the world of sinful kings.
- Rama - The ideal human being.
- Krishna - The mediator and politician.
- Buddha - The promoter of nonviolence (Ahimsa).
- Kalki - Due to come at the age end of decline of virtuous conduct.

Some Popular Bhagavan Vishnu Mantras

i) Shanta karam bhujag shayanam

The Mantra

*Om (Aum) shanta karam bhujag shayanam,
*padma nabham surehsham;
*vishva dharam gagana sadrusham,
*megha varnam shubhangam;
*Lakshmi kantam kamala nayanam,
*yogi bhir dhyan gamyam;
*vande Vishnum bhava bhaya haram,
*sarva loka eke naatham.

Word by word translation of this mantra

*Om (Aum) - the foremost name and symbol of The Lord. *shanta* - serene; *karam* - bearing and expression; *bhujag* - on serpents; *shayanam* - He who sleeps,

*padma - lotus shaped; *nabham* - navel; suresham - of all the demigods;

*vishva - the universe; *dharam* - holder of; *gagana* - above and beyond the clouds; *sadrusham* - whose vision exceeds,

*megha - changeable like the clouds in the sky; *varnam* - whose colour; *shubhangam* - whose body is completely auspicious;

*_Lakshmi_ - the expression of spiritual illumination; _kantam_ - the husband; _kamala_ - lotus flower; _nayanam_ - leading and managing,

*_yogi bhir_ - the yogis; _dhyan_ - through meditation; _gamyam_ - He who the yogis yearn to reach;

*_vande_ - I praise; _Vishnum_ - The Lord; _bhava_ - due to our inborn nature; _bhaya_ - fears; _haram_ - He who removes;

* _sarva_ - all; _loka_ - the world; _eka_ - one; _naatham_ - Lord.

General translation of this mantra

I offer my sincerest salutation and surrender to The Lord, who is serene in appearance, whose bed is the serpent Adishesha, whose navel is lotus shaped, who is The Lord of all the demigods, by whose grace this universe is maintained and protected, whose body is filled with auspiciousness, who is the beloved of Lakshmi Devi, whose eyes are like the lotus, who can only be reached by the yogis through meditation. I salute The Lord of the worlds and who is the remover of all fears.

Benefits of chanting this mantra

- This mantra purifies the mind thus making it receptive to Self-knowledge.
- It also graces the chanter with spiritual bliss.

Reference

Original source unknown.

ii) Om (Aum) Shuklam Bara Dharam Vishnum

The Mantra

Om (Aum) Shuklam ambara dharam Vishnum,
Shashi varnam chatur bhujam;
prassana vadanam dhyayeth,
sarva vighnopa shantaye.

Word by word translation of this mantra

Om (Aum) - The foremost name and symbol of The Lord; *shuklam* - white; *ambara* - dress; *dharam* - wearer; *Vishnum* - The all-pervading Lord,

Shashi - moonlight; *varnam* - colour; *chatur* - four; *bhujam* - arms;

prassana - smiling contentedly; *vadanam* – face; *dhyayeth* - I meditate,

sarva - all; *vighnopa* - barriers or obstacles; *shantaye* - remove or neutralize.

General translation of this mantra

I pray to The all-pervading Lord of this universe, the wearer of white clothes, whose appearance is bright like the moon, the possessor of four arms, smiling very contentedly, whose face radiates with a warm smile to remove all obstacles/barriers to this existence so that, I can maximize it to aid holistic growth.

Benefits of chanting this mantra

- Its chanting confers mental peace.

Reference

Original source unknown.

iii) Om (Aum) Yam Brahma

The mantra

Om (Aum) yam Brahma Varuna Indra Rudra Marutah,
stunvanti divyai stavai;
vedai sa anga pada krama upanisidhai,
gayanti yam samagah;
dhyana avasthita tat gatena manasa,
pashyanti yam yogino;
yasya antam na viduh sura asura gana,
Devai tasmai namah.

Word by word translation of this mantra

Om (Aum) - The foremost name and symbol of The Lord. *yam* - whom; *Brahma* - Brahma (The creator); *Varuna* - Varuna, the manager of water resources; *Indra* - The administer of heaven; *Rudra* - Lord Shiva; *marutah* - the maruts,

stunvanti - praise; *divyai* - unequalled; *stava*i - prayers;

vedai - all the vedas; *sa* - along; *anga* - corollary branches; *pada krama* - special sequential arrangements of mantras; *Upanisidha*i - all the Upanisad;

gayanti - sing about; *yam* - who; *samagah* - singers of the Sam veda,

*_dhyan_a - in meditation; _avasthita_ - situated; _tat_ - that; _gatena_ - which is fixed upon Him; _manasa_ - with the mind;

*_pashyanti_ - sees; _yam_ - whom; _yogino_ - the mystic yogis;

*_yasya_ - whose; _antam_ - end; _na_ - not; _viduh_ - they know; _sura_ - demi gods; _asura_ - demons; _gana_ - all;

*_Devai_ - The Supreme Lord; _tasmai_ - to Him; _namah_ - I offer my salutation and surrender.

General translation of this mantra

I offer my sincerest salutation and surrender to the Supreme Lord of the universe, who is praised by Brahma, Varuna, Indra and Rudra (Shiva - an expression of the Lord who is the annihilator of the universe at the end of the cycle of time) the maruts praise through the chanting of transcendental hymns and recitation of the Vedas, sequential arrangements of mantras, Upanishads and the chanter of the Sama Veda, who is seen by perfect yogis in trance. Your limits can never be seen by any member of your creation.

Benefits of chanting this mantra

- This mantra promotes spiritual growth.

Reference

Swami Prabhupada (1992)-Shreem Bhagavatam- Bhakti Vedanta Book Trust, Botany, New South Wales 2019, Australia-Canto 12, Chap 13, Verse 1.

iv) Om (Aum) Mangalam Bhagavan Vishnu

The mantra

*Om (Aum) mangalam Bhagavan Vishnu,
*mangalam Garuda dhvaja;
*mangalam pundari kaksha,
*mangalaya tanno Hari.

Word by word translation of this mantra

*Om (Aum) - The foremost name and symbol of The Lord. *mangalam* - auspiciousness; *Bhagavan* - The Lord who is the possessor of infinite fortune; *Vishnu* - The protector and maintainer of this Universe,

* *mangalam* - auspiciousness; *Garuda* - the king of birds and the vehicle of Lord Vishnu; *dhvaja* - flag;

**mangalam* - auspiciousness; *pundari* - lotus; *kaksha* - eyes,

**mangalaya* - auspiciousness; *tanno. Hari* - who is the abode of.

General translation of this mantra

The Lord who is the owner of all fortunes pervades, this entire world and its creation, is very auspicious. All auspiciousness to The Lord who has the king of birds Garuda as His flag. Auspiciousness to The Lord whose eyes are like the lotus flower. He (Lord Hari) is the abode of the source of all auspiciousness.

Benefits of chanting this mantra

- When chanted, this mantra seeks the aid of The Lord to bless the religious ceremony from commencement to the end.

Reference

Garuda Purana-Dharma Kanda, Chap 47.

v) Om (Aum) Apavitrah Pavitro

The Mantra

*Om (Aum) apavitrah pavitro va,
*sarva avasthanam gato pi va;
*ya smaret pundarika aksam,
*sa bahya abhyantarah shucih.

Word by word translation of this mantra

Om (Aum) - The foremost name and symbol of The Lord. *apavitrah* - impure; *pavitro* - pure; *va* - on one side,

sarva - the entire or whole; *avasthanam* - condition; *gato* - known or understood; *api* - move or go; *va* - either;

ya - mover or goer; *smaret* - remember; *pundarika* - white lotus flower; *aksam* - eyes,

sa - along with; *bahya* - external body; *abhyantarah* - internally I am Atma or Self or Soul; *shucih* - bestow purity on me.

General translation of this mantra

If one is impure or pure in any conditions of life, if he or she remembers The Lotus eyed Lord Vishnu, who is the maintainer and protector of this universe, he or she will be graced with material and spiritual purity.

Benefits of chanting this mantra
- This mantra will grace the life of the spiritual aspirant (sadhaka) with peace and purity of mind - a very necessary qualification to aid in spiritual growth

Reference

Lecture 1 December 1968, Angeles (http://www.prabhupadavani.org/main/lectures/vo 7.htm)

6 Bhagavan (The Lord) Sri Rama Namaskar (Salutations)

i) The word Rama

- **Ra** - means Rudra or Shiva (The expression of The Lord who deals with annihilation of the universe at the end of cycle).
- **Aa** - means Brahma (The expression of The Lord who is the source of creation of this universe).
- **Ma** - means Vishnu (The expression of The Lord which over sees maintenance and protection of this universe).

ii) The word Rama

- **Ra** - comes from the eight-syllable mantra of Narayana Na-**ra**-ya-na-ya.
- **Ma** - comes from the five syllabled Shiva mantra Na-**ma**-Shi-va-ya.

Effects of chanting the name Ra+Ma

- Destroys evil.
- Eradicates obstacles.
- Leads to liberation (mukti).

What is the meaning of the word Bhagavan?

One who has the six-fold virtues in absolute measure (**Bhaga**). The six-fold virtues are:

- **Jnana** (absolute knowledge).
- **Vairagya** (absolute detachment).
- **Virya** (the capacity to create, maintain and resolve).
- **Yashas** (absolute fame0.
- **Sri** (absolute wealth).
- **Aishwarya** (absolute over lordship).

What is the meaning of the word Sri?

Sri means the auspicious Lord.

Bhagavan Sri Rama is the most worshipped expression of The Lord

Known as Maryada Purushtotama (the perfect man or master of self-control and virtue) is the seventh (7th) avatar (descent into the material world), is the most worshipped expression of The Lord in Hinduism (Sanatan Dharma).

Some Popular Bhagavan Sri Rama Mantras

i) Om (Aum) Ramaya Rama Bhadraya

The Mantra

**Om (Aum) Ramaya Rama bhadraya,*
*Rama Chandraya vedhase;
*Raghu Nathaya Nathaya,
*Sita pataye namaha.

Word by word translation of this mantra

Om (Aum) - The foremost name and symbol of The Lord. *Ramaya* - The Lord who is the seventh avatar (descent of Vishnu - The lord of the world). *Rama* - The ideal human being; *bhadraya* - comfortable;

*Rama - The Lord who is the ideal human being; *Chandraya*- brighter than the moon; *vedhase* - Lord Brahman;

*Raghu - great grandfather of Sri Rama; *Nathaya* - Lord of; *Nathaya* - The Lord;

*Sita - Divine mother Sita (an expression of Lakshmi Devi); *Pataye* - Lord of; *namah* - I offer my sincerest salutation and surrender.

General translation of this mantra

I offer my sincerest salutation and surrender to Rama, Rama Bhadra and Raghunath (three names of Shri Rama, who is The Lord of the universe), who is brighter than the Moon and who, is the consort of mother Sita. You my Lord are the original Brahman (Lord of this universe).

Benefits of chanting this Mantra

- This mantra will aid in the chanter rising above the body/mind/intellect complex to be at one with the Aatma or the Self.

Reference

Padma Purana-Uttar Khanda Uma Maheshvara Sam Vada 254-261

Stotram 27-Sri Buddha Kaushika Rishi.

ii) Hare Rama

The Mantra

>*Hare Rama Hare Rama,
>*Rama Rama Hare Hare;
>*Hare Krishna Hare Krishna,
>*Krishna Krishna Hare Hare.

Word by word translation of this mantra

Hare - energy of The Supreme Lord; *Rama* - One whose mind is purified; *Hare* - one who removes our illusions; *Rama* - The embodiment of dharma (virtuous conduct);

Rama - the reservoir of pleasure; *Rama* - the bliss of the yogis; *Hare* - one who pulls us to Him; *Hare* - one who drives away barriers to our spiritual growth;

Hare - energy of The Supreme Lord; *Krishna* - the all attractive Lord; *Hare* - one who removes our illusions; *Krishna* - one who is the boon giver;

Krishna - the refuge of the destitutes; *Krishna* - one who liberates us; *Hare* - who pulls us to Him; *Hare* - one who drives away barriers to spiritual growth.

General translation of this mantra

Oh, Supreme energy, whose mind is pure, the remover of our illusions, the embodiment of dharma (virtuous conduct), the reservoir of pleasure, the bliss of the yogis, who is all attractive, the boon giver, refuge of the destitutes, the liberator. Let my life be free of barriers so that I can engage myself in your loving service.

Benefits of chanting this mantra

- It increases bhakti or devotion to the Lord.
- It destroys the adverse effects of this age of Kali.

Reference

Kali Santara Upanisad.

iii) Tvam eva mata

The Mantra

> *Tvam eva mata cha pita tvam eva,
> *tvam eva bandhu cha sakha tvam eva;
> *tvam eva vidya dravinam tvam eva,
> *tvam eva sarvam mama deva deva.

Word by word translation of this mantra

*Tvam - you; eva - alone; mata - mother; cha - and; pita - father; tvam - you; eva - alone;

*tvam - you; eva - alone; bandhu - relations; cha - and; sakha - eternal friend; tvam - you; eva - alone;

*tvam - you; eva - alone; vidya - my source of education; dravinam - highest wealth; tvam - you; eva - alone;

*tvam - you; eva - alone; sarvam - all-in-all; mama - my soul; Deva - The ultimate Lord; Deva - the perfect supreme Lord.

General translation of this mantra

You alone my Lord of Lord are my mother, father, relations, eternal friend, source of my education and highest spiritual wealth; all-in-all my Lord of Lord you are my Atma or soul.

Benefits of chanting this mantra

- When one is feeling low and dejected chanting this mantra is a reminder that The lord can be relied upon to lift us up.
- It is a mantra of complete surrender to the Divine will of The Lord.

Reference

Pandava gita - verse 28 - chanted by Gandhari (wife of Dhrtarastra) to seek kinship with Shri Krishna

iv) Ram Rameti Rameti

The Mantra

Ram Rameti Rameti,
Rame Rame manorame;
sahastra naam tat tulyam,
Ram naam varanine.

Word by word translation of this mantra

Ram - Sri Rama (the seventh avatar of Lord Vishnu); *Rameti* - saying Ram; *Rameti* - saying Ram,

Rame - pleasing; *Rame* - unto Ram; *manorame* - lovely;

sahastra - one thousand; *naam* - names; *Tat* - that; *tulyam* - equivalent or comparable;

Ram - Sri Rama; *naam* - name of; *varanane* - the best.

General translation of this mantra

Oh, fair faced Parvati, I enjoy reciting Lord Rama's name; by uttering His glorious name but once, this is equivalent to the recitation of the thousand names of Lord Vishnu.

Benefits of chanting this Stotram (a eulogy or a hymn of praise)

- The spiritual aspirant gains the protection of The Lord.
- It aids spiritual growth.

Reference

Shri Budha Kaushika Rishi-Ram Raksha Stotram - Stotra 38

7 Sri Hanuman Ji Namaskar (Salutations)

Who is Hanuman?

Hanuman is an avatar (descent of Lord Shiva who is an Expression of Lord Vishnu. Shiva is responsible for the annihilation of this universe at the end of its cycle).

Parentage of Lord Hanuman

- His Mother is Anjani Devi.
- His father is Vayu Deva (Wind God).

Origin of the name Hanuman

- Hanu - Jaw.
- Man - Swollen.

What is the meaning of Sri and Ji?

Sri means the auspicious Lord. **Ji** is a term of exceedingly high respect.

Devotee of Bhagavan Sri Rama

Lord Hanuman is the dearest devotee of Sri Ramachandra and as a result, He is the central character in the Ramayana. It is also to be noted, that He is mentioned in the Mahabharat.

He is renowned for being The Lord of:
- Knowledge.
- Intelligence.
- Immeasurable strength.
- Destroyer of obstacles

Some Popular Sri Hanuman Ji's Mantras

i) Om (Aum) atulita bal dhaaman

The Mantra

Om (Aum) atulita bal dhaaman,
hem shailabh deham,
danuja van kruishanam;
gyanaani naam agraganyam,
sakal gun nidhaanam;
vaanar naam dheesham,
Raghu pati priya bhaktam;
vaat jaatam namami.

Word by word translation of this mantra

Om (Aum) - The foremost name and symbol of The Lord. *atulita bal dhaaman* - one who is the reservoir of unequalled power and strength;

hem shailabh deham - one whose body resembles a golden mountain,

danuja van kruishanam - the destroyer of demonic forces

gyani naam agraganyam - the chief amongst the knowledgeable and self-realized;

sakal guna nidhaanam - the store house of virtuous values;

vaanar naam dheesham - chief of the monkeys;

Raghu pati bhaktam - the dearest devotee of Lord Rama;

* *Vaat jaatam namami* - my salutations to Shri Hanuman.

General translation of this mantra

I offer my sincerest salutations and surrender to Lord Hanuman, the reservoir of unequalled strength, whose body resembles a golden mountain, the destroyer of demonic forces, chief amongst the knowledgeable and self-realized, the storehouse of virtuous values and the dearest devotee of Lord Rama.

Benefits of chanting this mantra

- Makes one victorious over difficulties.
- Aids in acquisition of material and spiritual knowledge.

Reference

Original source unknown.

ii) Om (Aum) Hanuman Ji Namah

The Mantras

Om (Aum) Hanuman Ji namah,
Om (Aum) Anjani soonah namah;
Om (Aum) Vayu putra namah,
Om (Aum) maha bala namah;
Om (Aum) Ramestha namah,
Om (Aum) Phalgun sakha namah;
Om (Aum) amita vikramah namah,
Om (Aum) ping akscha namah;
Om (Aum) uddadhi kramana namah,
Om (Aum) Sita shoka vinashana namah;
Om (Aum) Lakshman prana data namah,
Om (Aum) dasha griva darpaha namah.

Word by word translation of these twelve Mantras

Om (Aum) - the foremost name and symbol of The Lord. *Hunuman Ji namah* - my salutation to the Supreme spirit,

Om (Aum) - The Lord; *Anjani soonah namah* - My salutation to the son of Anjani Devi;

Om (Aum) - The Lord; *Vayu putra* namah - my salutation to the son of Vayu Deva,

Om (Aum) - The Lord: *maha bala namah* - my salutation to the one of great strength;

Om (Aum) - The Lord; *Ramestha namah* - my salutation to the devotee of Shri Rama,

* *Om (Aum)* - The Lord; *Phalguna sakha namah* - my salutation to the friend of Arjuna;

**Om (Aum)* - The Lord; *ping akscha namah* - my salutation to the one with brown eyes,

**Om (Aum)* - The Lord; *amita vikramah namah* - my salutation to your infinite bravery;

**Om (Aum)* - The Lord: *uddadhi kramanah namah* - my salutation to you my Lord who has crossed the ocean,

**Om (Aum)* - The Lord; *Sita shoka vinashana namah* - my salutation to the remover of the sorrow of mother Sita;

**Om (Aum)* - The Lord; *Lakshman prana data namah* - my salutation to the restorer of Lakshmana's life,

**Om (Aum)* - The Lord; *dash griva darpana namah* - my salutation to the destroyer the ten headed ego or pride.

General translation of these twelve mantras

I offer my sincerest salutation and surrender to the lotus feet of The Supreme Lord, the son of Anjani Devi and Vayu Deva, the one with great strength, the devotee par excellence of Shri Rama, friend of Arjuna of the famous Mahabharata, the one with brown eyes and who is extremely brave, the one who has crossed the ocean, the remover of mother Sita's sorrow, the restower of Lakshmana's life and the destroyer of the ten headed ego or pride(Ravana).

Benefits of chanting these twelve mantras

- The chanting of these twelve mantras will make one victorious over one's enemies.

Reference

Original source unknown.

iii) Manojavam Maruta Tulya vegam

The Mantra

*Om (Aum) manojavam Maruta tulya vegam,
*jitendriyam buddhimataam varistham;
*vataatmajam vaanara yootha mukhyam,
*Shri Raama dootam sharanam prapadye.

Word by word translation of this mantra

Om (Aum) - the foremost name and symbol of The Lord. *manojavam* - as swift as the mind; *Maruta* - the wind; *tulya vegam* - more powerful than,

jitendriyam - the conqueror of the mind; *buddhimataam* - one whose excellence is recognized; *varistham* - one who is intelligent and learned;

vataatmajam - the supreme amongst all intelligent being; *vaanara* - forest creatures; *yootha* - army of; *mukhyam* - commander,

Shri - title of respect; *Raama* - Lord Raama; *dootam* - servant of; *sharanam* - refuge or shelter; *prapadye* - I prostrate myself at your lotus feet.

General translation of this mantra

I offer my sincerest salutation and surrender to the lotus feet of Lord Hanuman (an expression of Lord Shiva), who is as swift as the human mind, as fast as the wind, the master of His senses, revered for His excellence in education, and wisdom. I seek refuge in the son of the wind God, commander of the army of forest creatures and devotee of Shri Rama (The seventh avatar - descent into this material world of Lord Vishnu).

Benefits of chanting this mantra

This mantra will grace the chanter with victory in overcoming problems e.g.:

- Psychological.
- Physical.
- Social.

Reference
Sri Budha Kaushika Rishi-Stotram 33.

8 Bhagavan (The Lord) Sri Krishna Namaskar (Salutations)

Who is Bhagavan Sri Krishna?

Sri Krishna is the eight avatar (descent into the material world of Bhagavan Vishnu The Lord of this universe).

What is the meaning of Bhagavan?

One who has the six-fold virtues in absolute measure (**Bhaga**). The six-fold virtues are:
- **Jnana** (absolute knowledge).
- **Vairagya** (absolute detachment).
- **Virya** (capacity to create, maintain and resolve).
- **Yashas** (absolute fame).
- **Sri** (absolute wealth).
- **Aishwarya** (absolute over lordship).

Bhagavan Sri Krishna is the embodiment of;

- Care.
- Tenderness.
- Love.

Bhagavan Sri Krishna is the central character in:

- The Mahabharata.
- Shrimad Bhagavatam (Bhagavat Purana).
- Shrimad Bhagavad Gita.

Meaning of the name Krishna

- **Krish** - the attractive feature of absolute existence (Sat).
- **Na** - that which is spiritual bliss.

Some Popular Bhagavan Sri Krishna Mantras

i) Om (Aum) Namo Bhagavate Vasudevaya

The Mantra

Om (Aum)
Namo,
Bhagavate,
Vasudevaya.

Word by word translation of this mantra

Om (Aum) - The foremost name and symbol of The Lord.

Namo - I offer my sincerest salutation and surrender,

Bhagavate - The Divine Lord,

Vasudevaya - son of Vasudeva.

General translation of this mantra

I offer my sincerest salutation and surrender to the lotus feet of the son of Vasudeva, who is The Lord of this world.

Benefits of chanting this mantra

- Aids spiritual development.
- It can in the course of time lead to liberation (moksha).

Reference

Swami Dayananda Saraswati (2004) - Om Namo Bhagavat Vasudevaya - Arsha Vidya Gurukulum, Coimbatore, 641 108, Tamil Nadu, India.

ii) Om Vasudeva Sutam Devam

The Mantra

Om (Aum) Vasudeva sutam Devam,
Kamsa chanoora mardanam;
Devaki Parama Anandam,
Krishna vande jagat Gurum.

Word by word translation of this mantra

Om (Aum) - The foremost name and symbol of The Lord. *Vasudeva* - Sri Krishna's father/the life in all beings; *sutam* - son; *Devam* - The Supreme Lord,

Kamsa - Sri Krishna's mother's brother; *Chanoora* - a wrestler in Kamsa's court; *Mardanam* - kill;

Devaki - Sri Krishna's mother; *Parama* – The Supreme; *Anandam* - bliss,

Krishna - Sri Krishna; *vande* - my sincerest salutation; *jagat* - the world; *Gurum* - The Acharya or Spiritual master.

General translation of this mantra

I offer my sincerest salutation and surrender to The Spiritual Master of the world, the destroyer of Kamsa and Chanoora and the source of Supreme Bliss for His Mother.

Benefits of chanting this mantra

- It praises the bravery and glory of The Lord.
- Aids in the relief of stress.

Reference

Swami Dayananda Saraswati (2006) - Bhagavad Gita (Home Study Course) - Arsha Vidya Gurukulum, Coimbatore, 641 108, Tamil Nadu, India - Vol 1, Gita Dhyanam, Verse 5.

iii) Om (Aum) Mukam Karoti Vacalam

The Mantra

*Om (Aum) mukam karoti vacalam,
*pangum langhayate girim;
*yat kripa tam aham vande;
*Param Ananda Madhavan.

Word by word translation of this mantra

Om (Aum) - the foremost name and symbol of The Lord. *mukam* - mute or dumb; *karoti* - makes; *vacalam* - eloquent,

pangum - lame; *langhayate* - cross; *girim* - mountain;

yat - whose; *kripa* - grace; *tam* - Him; *aham* - I; *Vande* - salute,

Param - infinite; *Ananda* - bliss; *Madhavan* - Shri Krishna

General translation of this mantra

I offer my sincerest salutation to The Lord of Infinite bliss, Shri Krishna, the deliverer of fallen embodied living beings (jivas), by whose grace the mute excels in speech and who enables the lame to climb mountains.

Benefits of chanting this mantra
- It aids in development of firm faith in God.
- It develops a positive mental attitude.

Reference

Swami Prabhupada (1992) - Shreemad Bhagavatam-Bhakti Vedanta Book Trust, Bombay 400 049, India - Canto 6, Chap. 7, Verse 23.

Swami Dayananda Saraswati (2006) - Bhagavad-Gita (Home Study Course) - Arsha Vidya Gurukulum, Coimbatore 641108, Tamil Nadu, India - Vol 1, Geeta Dhyanam, Verse 8.

iv) Om (Aum) Kaayena Vaaca

The Mantra

*Om (Aum) kaayena vaachaa manas endriyair va,
*buddhya atmanaa va anusrta svabhaavaat;
*karoti yad yat sakalam parasmai,
*Narayana ya iti samarpayet.tat.

Word by word translation of this mantra

Om (Aum) - The foremost name and symbol of The Lord, *kaayena* - with my entire body; vaachaa - speech; *manas* - mind; *endriyair* - senses; *va* - or,

buddhyaat - with intelligence; *atmanaa* - with consciousness; *va* - or; *anusrta* - followed; *svabhaavaat* - my inner nature;

karoti - one does; *yat* - over; *yat* - over; *sakalam* - all; *Parasmai* - to the Supreme,

Narayana ya iti - This is for The Lord; *samarpayet.tat* - I dedicate all these actions to The Lord.

General translation of this mantra

In accordance with the particular nature one has acquired in life, all actions performed with this on loan body, speech, mind, intellect, senses and jivaatma (embodied soul), should be offered to the Supreme Lord for His Divine pleasure.

Benefits of Chanting this mantra

- It promotes spiritual growth via complete surrender of everything one has to The Lotus Feet of The Lord.

Reference

Swami Prabhupada (1992) Shreemad Bhagavatam- Bhakti Vedanta Book Trust, Bombay, 400 049, India - Canto11, Chap 2, Verse 36.

9 Bhagavan (The Lord) Shiva Namaskar (Salutations)

Meaning of the name Shiva

The name Shiva means:

- **Satyam** - absolute existence.
- **Shivam** - auspicious.
- **Sundaram** - beautiful.
- **Madhuram** - sweet.
- **Anandam** - blissful.

Role of Shiva

- Lord of compassion.
- Protector of devotees from internal and external enemies.
- Aids in liberation (moksha).

Bhagavan Shiva is the expression of The lord

Bhagavan Shiva is the expression of The Lord, who is responsible for the reabsorption of this universe at the end of its life cycle.

Some popular Bhagavan Shiva mantras

i) Om (Aum) Trayam Bhakam Yajamahe

The Mantra

>*Om (Aum); trayam bakam yajamahe,
>*sugandhim pushti vardhanam;
>*urvarukam eva bandhanam,
>*mrityor mukshaye ma amritat.

Word by word translation of this mantra

Om (Aum) - The foremost name and symbol of The Lord; *trayam* - three; *bakam* - eyes; *yajamahe* - we praise, honour and worship,

sugandhim - the joy that we get on knowing and seeing your virtuous deeds; *pushti* - one who nourishes; *vardhanam* - understanding and spiritual growth;

urvarukam - deadly and over powering diseases; *eva* - like, *bandhanam* - bondage,

mrityor - from death; *mukshaye* - liberate; *ma* - may I never again; *amritat* - freedom from limitations that I am this body-mind-intellect complex.

General translation of this mantra

I praise, honour, and worship The Three Eyed Lord; I am joyful on knowing and seeing your virtuous deeds, who nourishes my knowledge and spiritual growth. Please liberate me from the disease of attachment which binds me to this cycle of birth and death (samsara) so that I can be at one with my real nature i.e. Atma or Soul.

Benefits of chanting this mantra

- Makes one fearless.
- Heals and rejuvenate one's life.
- Grants liberation i.e. moksha.

Reference

Rig Veda - 7:59:12.

Swami Dayananda Saraswati (2011) - Shree Rudram - Arsha Vidya Research and Publication Trust, Chennai 600 004, India - Anuvaaka 11.

ii) Om (Aum) Na Ma Shi Va Ya

The mantra
*Om (Aum), * Na, * Ma, * Shi, * Va, * Ya*

Word by word translation of this mantra

Om (Aum) - The foremost name and symbol of The Lord.

Na - is The Lord's concealing grace, it also represents the earth.

Ma - represents this world as well as water.

Shi - is Lord Shiva (The expression of The Lord who reabsorbs this universe at the end of the cycle of time). Shi also means fire.

Va - Is the revealing grace of The Lord as well as the Pranic air (The life force or vital principle which energizes and elivens our existence).

Ya - is the Self, Soul or the atman. Ya is also the sky or akash.

General translation of this mantra

With all humility, I bow down to The Supreme Lord Shiva who is Om (Aum), The Inner Self, that consciousness which dwells in all members of creation.

Benefits of chanting this mantra

- It calms the mind.
- It graces the spiritual aspirant (sadhaka) with freedom from physical and mental diseases.
- Aids Lord Shiva's protection to his sincere devotees (bhaktas).

Reference

Swami Dayananda Saraswati (2011) - Shree Rudram - Arsha Vidya Research Publication Trust, Chennai 600 004, India - Anuvaaka 8.

iii) Om (Aum) Namah Shambhave Cha

The Mantra

Om (Aum) namah shambhave ca,
*mayobhave ca;
*namah shankaraya ca,
*mayaskaraya ca;
*namah shivaaya ca,
*Shivataraya ca.

Word by word translation of this mantra

Om (Aum) - The foremost name and symbol of The Lord *namah* - Salutation and surrender) *shambhave* - the one who makes us happy here in this existence; *ca* - and,

*mayobhave - the one who makes us happy in the hereafter; *ca* - and;

*namah - my salutation and surrender; *Shankaraya* - The Lord who is the source of happiness; *ca* - and,

*mayaskaraya - The Lord who makes free from limitations; *ca* - and;

*namah - salutation and surrender; *shivaaya* - Lord Shiva; *ca* - and,

*shivataraya - The One who gives total happiness; ca - and.

General translation of this mantra

O Divine Lord Shiva, you are the supreme source of all pleasures and holistic growth. We offer our sincerest salutation and surrender to your lotus feet.

Benefits of chanting this mantra

- By chanting this mantra, the innermost wishes of the spiritual aspirant (sadhaka) is fulfilled.
- The devotee of this mantra is assured of Lord Shiva's divine protection.

Reference

Swami Dayananda Saraswati (2011) - Shree Rudram - Arsha Vidya Research and Publication Trust, Chennai 600 004, India - Anuvaakya 8, Page 177.

iv) Om (Aum) Kara Charana Krtam Vak

The Mantra

Om (Aum) kara charana krtam vak,
kayajam karmajam va;
shravana nayanajam va,
maanasam va aparadham;
vihitam avihitam va,
sarvame Tat kshamasva;
jaya jaya karunabdhe,
Sri Mahadeva Shambho.

Word by word translation of this mantra

Om (Aum) - The foremost name and symbol of The Lord, kara - hands; *charana* - feet; *krtam* - done; *vak* - speech,

kaya - this physical body; *jam* - borne out; *karma* - actions; *jam* - borne out; *va* - or;

shravana - hearing or listening; *nayana* - eyes and ears; *jam* - borne out; *va* - or,

maanasam - mind; *va* - or; *aparadham* - mistakes;

vihitam - good actions without thinking; *avihitam* - illegal actions; *va* - or,

sarvam - all; *etat* - these; *kshamasva* - forgive;

jaya - victory or glory; *jaya* - victory or glory; *karuna* - kindness; *abdhe* - ocean,

Sri - radiant holiness; *Mahadeva* - Lord Shiva (the great); *Shambho* - the cause of happiness.

General translation of this mantra

Lord, please forgive me for actions performed by my eyes, ears, mind, organ of speech, hands and feet without good thinking legally or illegally. Glory, glory to you my Lord of compassion, kindness and happiness

Benefits of chanting this mantra

- This mantra is chanted to seek forgiveness from The Lord, for appropriate actions carried out thoughtlessly and for sinful action(s).

Reference
http://hindudevotionalstotram.blogspot.in

v) Om (Aum) Karpur Gauram

The Mantra

Om (Aum) karpur gauram karuna avataram,
sansaar saaram bhujagendra haram;
sadaa vasantam hrdaya aravinde,
bhavam bhavaanee sahitam namami.

Word by word translation of this mantra

Om (Aum) - The foremost name and symbol of The Lord, *karpur* - camphor; *gauram* - as pure as; *karuna* - compassion; *avataram* - descent of full,

sansaar - the world; *saaram* - the one who is the essence; *bhujagendra* - the one with the serpent king; *haram* - his garland;

sadaa - always; *vasantam* - residing; *hrdaya* - heart; *aravinde* - lotus,

bhavam - to the Lord; *bhavaanee* - wife of Lord Shiva; *sahitam* - to you both; *namami* - I bow.

General translation of this mantra

I offer my sincerest surrender to Lord Shiva and mother Sati, the avatar (descent into this material world) of compassion, the essence of this material existence, pure like white camphor, whose garland is the king of serpents, whose abode is the lotus of the heart.

N.B. Lord Shiva and Mother Sati are one.

Benefits of chanting this mantra

- Aids protection from enemies and dangers.

Reference

http://www.youtube.com/TheMeditativeMind

vi) Om (Aum) Guru Brahma

The Mantra

Om (Aum) Guru Brahma,
Guru Vishnu;
Guru Devo Maheshvara,
Guru Sakshat Para Brahma;
tasmai Shri Guruve namah.

Word by word translation of this mantra

Om (Aum) - The foremost name and symbol of The Lord. *Gu* - one who is above the qualities of the mind (sattva-mode of goodness, rajas-mode of passion and activity, tamas-mode of ignorance) *ru*- The lord who is formless (Nirguna Brahman); *Brahma* - The one God who is called Brahma when He creates this world,

Guru - The Lord who is above the qualities of the mind; *Vishnu* - The one god who is called Vishnu when He maintains and protect this world;

Guru - The Lord who is above the qualities of the mind; *Devo* - God; *Maheshvara* - The one God who reabsorbs this world at the end of the cycle of time,

Guru - The lord who is above the qualities of the mind; *Sakshat* - Himself; *Para* - the infinite; *Brahma* - Lord;

tasmai - to such; *Shri* - the holy radiance who removes my ignorance; *Guruve* - unto you my Lord; *namah* - I offer my sincerest salutation and surrender

General translation of this mantra

I offer my humblest salutation and surrender to my Lord God, who is above the qualities of the mind (gunatita), who is formless (Nirguna), who expresses Himself as the creator-Brahma, the maintainer and the protector Vishnu and Shiva the reabsorber of this world at the end of the cycle of time. May my Lord God free me from the ignorance of forgetfulness of my real nature which is **The Atma or Soul.**

Benefits of chanting this mantra

- This mantra aids in the process of spiritual growth and liberation (moksha).

Reference

Baba Shri Shri Muralidharan Ji (date unknown) - Shree Guru Gita - Baba Shri Shri Muralidharan Ji, Calcutta 700 029, India - Verse 32, Page 53-55.

10 Sri Durga Devi (Divine Mother) Namaskar (Salutations)

Meaning of the name Durga

Durga refers to the Lord who is invincible.

- **Du-**poverty, suffering, famine and evil habits.
- **R-**disease.
- **Ga-**The destroyer of poverty, sufferings, famine, evil habits c disease and. sin

Who is Durga?

Durga is the expression of the one God who provides the energy for the dissolution and recreation of this universe.

Durga is referred to as

- Durgatinashinini-the one who eliminates suffering.
- Shakti or Devi.

Reference

Original source unknown.

Some Popular Sri Durga Devi Mantras

i) Om (Aum) sarva mangal mangalye

The Mantra

>*Om (Aum) sarva mangal mangalye
>*Shive sarva artha sadhike,
>*sharanye Trayambake Gauri
>*Narayaani namo stute.

Word by word translation of this mantra

Om (Aum) - The foremost name and symbol of The Lord. *sarva* - all; *mangal* - auspicious; *mangalye* - of all that is auspicious

Shive - consort of Lord Shiva; *sarva* - all; *artha* - wealth; *sadhike* - accomplishing desires,

sharanye - the refuge of all; *trayambake* - the three eyed Lord Shiva; *Gauri* - the one whose complexion is fair;

Narayaani - Mother Durga; *namo* - salutation; *stute* - unto you.

General translation of this mantra

I offer my sincerest salutation and surrender to Mother Durga, the auspiciousness of all that is auspicious, The consort of Lord Shiva, the ocean of accomplishments and the refuge of all.

Benefits of chanting this mantra

- It graces the chanter with wisdom.
- It aids in the development of a prosperous life.

Reference

Devadatta Kalee (2003) - Devee Maahaatmyam (In praise of The Goddess) - Motilal Banarsidas, Delhi 110 007, India - The Shree Durga Sapta Shloka Stotra, Verse 3, Page 34.

ii) Om (Aum) Jayanti Mangala Kali

The Mantra

>*Om (Aum) jayanti mangala,*
>*bhadra kali kapalini;*
>*Durga Shiva kshma dhatri,*
>*svaha svadha namo stute.*

Word by word translation of this mantra

Om (Aum) - The foremost name and symbol of The Lord, *jayanti* - always victorious; *mangala* - giver of auspiciousness;

kali - Lord of time; *bhadrakali* - Lord of life and death; *kapalini* - the wearer of a garland of skulls,

Durga - Goddess Durga; *Shiva* - the auspicious one; *kshma* - embodiment of patience; *dhatri* - the supporter of all members of creation;

svaha - the final receiver of the sacrificial oblations to the Gods; *svadha* - the final receiver of the oblations to the manes; *namo* - salutations; *stute* - unto you.

General translation of this mantra

I offer my sincerest salutation and surrender to the ever victorious, the giver of auspiciousness, The Lord or time, The Lord of life and death, the wearer of a garland of skulls, Mother Durga - The auspicious one, who is patient, the supporter of all members of creation, the receiver of the oblations for the Gods and the receiver of the oblations for all the departed.

Benefits of chanting this mantra

- Aids in problem solving.
- Confers power and strength.

Reference

Chaturvedi B.K. (1996) – Durga (Gods and Goddesses of India 7) - D.K. Publishers Distributors (P) Ltd, New Delhi 110 002, India - Page 61.

iii) Nava (nine) Durga Mantras

The Mantras

*Om (Aum) Shailputri namah.
*Om (Aum)Brahamachaarini namah.
*Om (Aum) Chandraghantaa namah.
*Om (Aum) Kushmanda namaha.
*Om (Aum) Skanda Mata namaha.
*Om (Aum) Kaataayani namaha.
*Om (Aum) Kaalaraatree namah
*Om (Aum) Maha Gauri namah.
*Om (Aum) Siddhi daatri namah.

Word by word translation of these twelve mantras

*Om (Aum) - the foremost name and symbol of The Lord; *Shailputri* - Daughter of the Himalayas; *namah* - my salutation and surrender,

*Om (Aum) - The Lord; *Brahamachaarini* - one who is celibate when doing penance; *namah* - my salutation and surrender;

*Om (Aum) - The Lord; *Chandraghantaa* - one whose necklace is adorned with the moon; *namah* - my salutation and surrender,

*Om (Aum) - The Lord; *Kushmanda* - The creator of this universe; *namah* - my salutation and surrender;

*_Om_ (Aum) - The Lord; _Skanda Mata_ - mother of Skanda; _namah_ - my salutation and surrender,

*_Om_ (Aum) - The Lord; _Kaataayani_ - the daughter of sage Katyaayana; _namah_ - my salutation and surrender;

*_Om_ (Aum) - The Lord; _Kaalaraatree_ - the destroyer of Kaali; _namah_ - my salutation and surrender,

*_Om_ (Aum) - The Lord; _Maha Gauri_ - wife of Lord Shiva; _namah_ - my salutation and surrender;

*_Om_ (Aum) - The Lord; _siddhi_ - provider of the siddhis; _daatri_ - mystic powers; _namah_ - my salutation and surrender.

General translation of this mantra

I offer my sincerest salutation and surrender to The Lord, who is the daughter of the Himalayas, who is celibate during penance, the wearer of a necklace with the moon on it, the creator of the universe, Mother of Skanda, daughter of sage Katyaayana, The destroyer of the age of kali, wife of Lord Shiva and the bestower of mystic powers.

Benefits of chanting these twelve mantras

- They provide protection form fire, enemies and grave crisis.

Reference

Devadatta Kaali (2003) - Deveemaahaatmyam (In praise of the Goddess) - Motilal Banarsidas, Delhi 110 007, India - Devyaah Kavacam, verses 1 to 8.

iv) Om (Aum) Sarva Swaroope Sarveshe

The Mantra

*Om (Aum) sarva swaroope sarveshe,
*sarva shakti samanvite;
*bhaye bhyastrahino devi,
*Durga Devi namo stute.

Word by word translation of this mantra

Om (Aum) - the foremost name and symbol of The Lord. *Sarva* - all; *swaroope* - one's own form or nature; *sarveshe* - omnipresent,

sarva - all; *shakti* - power; *samanvite* - everything;

bhaya - fear; *bhyastrahino* - eliminator of; *devi* - goddess,

Durga - Divine mother of the world; *Devi* - Goddess; *namah* - my salutation and surrender; *stute* - unto you.

General translation of this mantra

I offer my sincerest salutation and surrender to the Divine Mother of the world, who is omnipresent, who is the power in all, the eliminator of all fears.

Benefits of chanting this mantra

- This mantra removes all fears from one's life.

Reference

Original source unknown.

v) Om (Aum) Aim Hreem Kleem

The Mantra

Om (Aum) Aim hreem kleem,
Chamundaye vichche.

Word by word translation of this mantra

Om (Aum) - the foremost name and symbol of The Lord, *Aim* - is the seed mantra of Maha Saraswati (the expression of The Lord who is the overseer of knowledge needed for creation to take place); *hreem* - is the seed mantra of Maha Lakshmi (the expression of The Lord who provides resources for the maintenance of this universe), *kleem* - is the seed mantra of Maha Kali (the expression of The Lord responsible for power and death),

Chamundaye - Mother Durga, the protector of our lives, *vichche* - divine consciousness.

General translation of this mantra

I seek Mother Durga's blessings in the form of Maha Saraswati (the Lord of knowledge), Maha Lakshmi (The Lord of resources) and Maha Kali (The Lord of power and death), to strength our spiritual energy.

Benefits of chanting this mantra

- It makes one very positive.
- It increases the holistic strength of the individual.

Reference

Original source unknown.

11 Surya Devata (Lord) Namaskar (Salutation)

Who is Surya Devata?

Surya is the Sanskrit word for The Sun. He is the head of the nine (nav) planets (graha).

Synonyms of Surya Devata

Vishnu, Shakra, Aryamaa, Dhaataa, Tvastaa, Pooshaa, Vivasvan, Savitaa, Mitra, Varuna, Amsha, Bhaga.

Role of Surya Devata

Lord Surya is the expression of the one God whose roles are:

- Spiritual father of all God's creation.
- He represents the Aatma or Soul.
- Source of physical and spiritual illumination.
- Confers piety, truth and goodness.

Reference

Bisnauth R. (2018) - Hinduism (Sanatan Dharma) For the Enthusiastic Novice - R. Bisnauth - Chap 6.

Some Popular Surya Devata Mantras

i) Surya Namaskar Mantras

The Mantras

Om (Aum) Mitraya namah.
Om (Aum) Ravaye namah.
Om (Aum) Suryaya namah.
Om (Aum) Bhanave Namah.
Om (Aum) Khagaya namah.
Om (Aum) Pushne namah.
Om (Aum) Hiranyagarbhaya namah.
Om (Aum) Marichaye namah.
Om (Aum) Adityaya namah.
Om (Aum) Savitre namah.
Om (Aum) Arkaya namah.
Om (Aum) Bhaskaraya namah.

Word by word translation of the twelve mantras of Surya Devata

*Om (Aum) - the foremost name and symbol of the Lord. *Mitraya* - who is friendly to all; *namah* - my salutation and surrender,

*Om (Aum) - The Lord; *Ravaye* - to the radiant one; *namah* - my salutation and surrender;

*Om (Aum) - The Lord; *Suryaya* - dispeller of universal darkness; *namah* - my salutation and surrender,

Om (Aum) - The Lord; *Khagaya* - the all-pervading one; *namah* - my salutation and surrender,

Om (Aum) - The Lord; *Pushne* - the nourisher; *namah* - my salutation and surrender.

Om (Aum) - The Lord; *Bhanave* - the illuminator; *namah* - my salutation and surrender;

Om (Aum) - The Lord; *Hiranyagarbhaya* - one who is golden in colour; *namah* - my salutation and surrender,

Om (Aum) - The Lord; *Marichaye* - The Lord of infinite rays; *namah* - my salutation and surrender;

Om (Aum) - The Lord; *Adityaya* - son of mother Aditi; *namah* - my salutation and surrender,

Om (Aum) - The Lord; *Savitre* - the giver of life; *namah* - my salutation and surrender;

Om (Aum) - The Lord; *Arkaya* - one who is praiseworthy; *namah* - my salutation and surrender,

Om (Aum) - The Lord; *Bhaskaraya* - Lord of wisdom and universal light; *namah* - my salutation and surrender.

General translation of the twelve mantras of Surya Devata

I offer my sincerest salutation and surrender to The Supreme Lord who is always friendly to all, full of confidence, radiance, who is the remover of universal darkness, the eternal source of illumination, the pervader of this universe, the source of nourishment for all members of His creation, who is golden in colour, whose rays are infinite, son of Mother Aditi, the giver of life, the one who is praiseworthy, Lord of wisdom and spiritual illumination.

Benefits of chanting these twelve mantras of Surya Devata

- They aid in development of concentration.
- They promote spiritual growth.

Reference

Swami Tattvavidananda Saraswati (2004) - Aaditya Hrdayam - D.K. Printworld (P) Ltd, New Delhi 110 015, India - Pages 69-74.

ii) Gayatri Mantra

The Mantra

Om (Aum)
Om (Aum) Bhur Bhuva Svah,
Om (Aum) Tat Savitur Varenyam;
Bhargo Devasya Dheemahi,
Dhiyo Nah Prachodayat.
Om (Aum)

Word by word translation of Gayatri Mantra

Om (Aum) - The foremost name and symbol of The Lord.

Om (Aum) - The Lord;
Bhur - The Self-existent Lord, this earth or physical plane;
Bhuva - The self-conscious Lord, sky or astral plane;
Svah - The all-pervading Lord who is the incarnation of happiness, heaven.

Om (Aum) - The Lord;
Tat - The Supreme (Para) Lord (Brahma);
Savitur - The sun which illuminates us;
Varenyam - The Lord who is best of the best;

Bhargo - The bestower of wisdom;
Devasya - The beautiful and playful Lord;
Dheemahi - we meditate;

Dhiyo - Intellect,
Yo - we direct our prayer;
Nah - for all members of your creation;
Prachodayata - may You stimulate, inspire and guide us.

Om (Aum) - The Lord.

General translation of Gayatri mantra

We meditate (*Dheemahi*) on Lord Surya who is the bestower of wisdom and liberation (*moksha*), The best of the best, the most beautiful, The illuminator, The source of this earth (*Bhuh*), the sky (*Bhuvah*) and the heaven (*Svah*). May that Supreme Lord *(Tat)* stimulate (*prachodayata*) our (*nah*) intelligence (*dhiyo*) so that our prayers (*yo*) can be beneficial to all members of creation.

Benefits of chanting The Gayatri mantra

- Its chanting promotes the welfare of all members of creation.
- It is the pathway to liberation (moksha)

Reference

Sad guru Sant Keshavadas (1994) - Gayatree: The Highest Meditation - Motilal Banarsidas, Delhi 110 007, India - Practice of Sandhyaa Vandana, Page 91.

Mahanidhi Swami (1998) - Gayatri: Mahima Madhuri - Mahanidhi Swami, ISKCON, Vrndavan, Uttar Pradesh, India - Pages 24-34.

Swami Mukhyaananda (Date unknown) - Om Gayatree and Sandhya - Ramakrishna Math, Madras 600 004, India - Pages 17-18.

iii) Om (Aum) Asato Maa Sadgamaya

The Mantra

Om (Aum) Asato maa sadgamaya,
tamaso maa jyotir gamaya;
mrityor maa gamaya.

Word by word translation of this mantra

Om (Aum) - The foremost name and symbol of The Lord;
Asato - from ignorance of not knowing my real nature i.e. I am Aatma;
Maa - me;
Sad - to knowing that I am The Aatma or Self;
Gamaya - lead me,

tamaso - from spiritual darkness;
Maa - me;
Jyotir - spiritual illumination;
Gamaya - lead me;

mrityor - from the death of this ksetram (body/mind/intellect);
Maa - me;
Amritam - everlasting existence
Gamaya - lead me.

General translation of this mantra

Lead me from the bondage of transitory existence of lower understanding to the eternal Self or Aatma which is my real nature. Free me from the ignorance that I am this ksetram (body/mind/intellect) and lead me to my real nature i.e. Aatma. Guide my exit from this cycle of birth, growth, diseases, defects, old age and death towards freedom from limitations i.e. moksha.

Benefits of chanting this mantra

- Its chanting leads to liberation from the cycle of birth and death (samsara) by those who are serious.

Reference

Swami Krishnananda (2006) - The Brhadaaranyaka Upanisad - Divine Life Society, Shivananda Nagar, 249 192, Uttaranchal, India - Verse 28, pages 77-83.

iv) Lokah Samastah Sukhino Bhavantu

The Mantra

Om (Aum) lokah samastah sukhino bhavantu

Word by word translation of this mantra

Om (Aum) - The foremost name and symbol of The Lord.
Lokah - the whole world;
Samastah - all members of The Lord's creation;
Sukhino - be joyful and free of sufferings;
Bhav - The Divine State
Antu - may it be so

General translation of this mantra

May all members of The Lord's creation be happy, joyful and free from sufferings. May our thoughts, words and actions contribute to this happiness and freedom for all.

Benefits of chanting this mantra

- This mantra seeks to promote the welfare of all members of The Lord's creation.

Reference

Original source unknown.

12 Shanti (Peace) Namaskar (Salutations)

i) Om (Aum) Sarvesham Svastir Bhavatu

The Mantra

*Om (Aum) sarvesham svastir bhavatu,
*sarvesham shaantir bhavatu;
*sarvesham poornam bhavatu,
*sarvesham mangalam bhavatu.

Word by word translation of this mantra

*Om (Aum) - The foremost name and symbol of The Lord; *sarvesham* - that all people; *svastir* - experience good health; *bhavatu* - may they,

*sarvesham - that all people; *shaantir* - experience peace; *bhavatu* - may they;

*sarvesham - that all people; *poornam* - complete fulfillment; *bhavatu* - may they,

*sarvesham - that all people; *mangalam* - experience auspiciousness and spiritual success; *bhavatu* - may they.

General translation of this mantra

Let it so be established (*bhavatu*), that all members of The Lord's creation (*sarvesham*), experience well-being (*svastir*); let us all experience peace (*shaantir*), let us all enjoy complete fulfillment of our desires *(poornam)*, let us all have an auspicious and prosperous life (*mangalam*).

Benefits of chanting this mantra

- It promotes peace of mind.

Reference

Original source unknown.

ii) Om (Aum) Sarve Bhavantu Sukhina

The Mantra

*Om (Aum) sarve bhavantu sukhina,
*sarve santu niraa mayaaah;
*sarve bhadrani pashyanti,
*maa kashchit duhkha bhaagbhavet;
*Om (Aum) shanti.
*Om (Aum) shanti.
*Om (Aum) Shanti.

Word by word translation of this mantra

*Om (Aum) - The foremost name and symbol of The Lord, *sarve* - all; *bhavantu* - be; *sukhina* - be happy and prosperous,

sarve - all; *santu* - be; *nir* - without; *amayah* - illness;

sarve - all; *bhadrani* - good; *pashyanti* - may see,

maa - not; *kashchit* - all; *duhkh* - sorrow or suffering; *Bhaag* - share; bhavet - have.

*Om (Aum) - The Lord,
shanti - protection from all harm emanating from the sky e.g. thunder, lightning and rain (*adhidaivica*);

*Om (Aum) - The Lord
shanti - protection from all harm emanating from this earth e.g. harm from others in the form of theft and murder (*Adhibhautica*).

*Om (*Aum) - The Lord

shanti – protect me from all harm emanating from within myself e.g. self-harm (*Adhyatmica*).

General translation of this mantra

May it so happen that all members of The Lord's creation, are happy, prosperous, free from diseases. May they be blessed with Divine eyes (*Divya chaksu*) so that they see The Lord in everyone and everything they look at.

Om (Aum) - The Lord; *shanti* - may The Lord protect us from all harm emanating from the sky in the form of thunder, lightning and floods etc. (*Adidaivika*).

Om (Aum) - The Lord; *shanti* - may The Lord protect us from all harm emanating from this earth e.g. murderer, theft and injury (*Adhibhautica*).

Om (Aum) - The Lord; *shanti* – May The Lord protect us from all forms of self-harm (*Adhyatmica*).

Benefits of chanting this mantra

- Aids in the development of a positive mental attitude towards one's self and others.

Reference

Original source unknown.

iii) Om (Aum) Saha Nau Avatu

The mantra

*Om (Aum) saha nau avatu,
*Saha nau bhunaktu;
*saha viryam kara avavahai,
*tejasvi nau adhi tama astu;
*maa vidvisa vahai.
*Om (Aum) shanti,
*Om (Aum) shanti,
*Om Aum) shanti.

Word by word translation of this mantra

*Om (Aum) - The foremost name and symbol of The Lord, saha - together; nau - both of us; avatu - be protected,

*saha - together; nau - both of us; bhunaktu - enjoy the bliss of knowledge;

*saha - together; viryam - energy; karaa - hand; vaavahai - employ,

*tejasvi - well studied; nau - both of us; adhi - intellect; tama - higher degree; astu - let it be;

*maa - never; vidvisa - jealous; vahai - with each other.

*Om (Aum) - The Lord,
shanti – protect me from all harm emanating from the sky e.g. thunder, lightning and rain (adhidaivica);

*Om (Aum) - The Lord

shanti - protect me from all harm emanating from this earth e.g. harm from others in the form of theft and murder (*Adhibhautica*).

**Om (*Aum) - The Lord
shanti - protect me from all harm emanating from within myself e.g. self-harm (*Adhyatmica*).

General translation of this mantra

May The Lord protect both of us (teachers and students). May He facilitate the sharing of our learning. May we always understand what we studied. May our learning always be fruitful, and may we never be jealous of each other.

Om (Aum) - The Lord; *shanti* - may The Lord protect us from all harm emanating from the sky in the form of thunder, lightning and floods etc. (*Adidaivika*).

Om (Aum) - The Lord; *shanti* - may The Lord protect us from all harm emanating from this earth e.g. murderer, theft and injury (*Adhibhautica*).

Om (Aum) - The Lord; *shanti* - May The Lord protect us from all forms of self-harm (*Adhyatmica*).

Benefits of chanting this mantra

- It promotes a sincere desire to acquire holistic knowledge.
- It seeks to promote the welfare of all members of The Lord's creation.

Reference

Swami Chinmayananda (2000) - Kathopanishad: A dialogue with death - CCMT, Mumbai 400 072, India - Peace Invocation.

Swami Lokeswarananda (2009) - Katha Upanisad - Rama Krishna Mission Institute of Culture, Kolkata 700 029, India - Invocation.

iv) Om (Aum) Dhyau Shanti

The Mantra

Om (Aum) dhyau shanti,
antariksha gvam shanti;
prithvi shanti,
apah shanti;
oshadhaya shanti,
vanaspatayah shanti;
vishve devah shanti,
Brahma shanti;
sarvam shanti,
shantir eva;
shanti sa ma,
shanti redhi;
Om (Aum)shanti,
Om shanti;
Om shanti,

Word by word translation of this mantra

Om (Aum) - the foremost name and symbol of The Lord; *dhyau* - heaven; *shanti* - peace;

antariksha - sky; *gvam* - unto *shanti* - peace,

prithvi - earth; *shanti* - peace;

apah - water; *shanti* - peace;

oshadhaya - herbs; *shanti* - peace;

vanaspatayah - trees; *shanti* - peace,

vishve - all; *deva* - demigods; *shanti* - peace;

Brahma - The transcendental Lord; *shanti* - peace;

sarvam - all; *shanti* - peace;

shantir - peace; *eva* - unto you,

shanti - peace; *sa ma* - may we realize,

shanti - peace; *redh*i - unto me;

Om (Aum) - The Lord,
shanti - protection from all harm emanating from the sky e.g. thunder, lightning and rain (*adhidaivica*);

Om (Aum) - The Lord
shanti - protection from all harm emanating from this earth e.g. harm from others in the form of theft and murder (*Adhibhautica*).

*Om (*Aum) - The Lord
shanti - all harm emanating from within myself e.g. self-harm (*Adhyatmica*).

General translation of this mantra

May there be peace in the heaven, peace in the entire sky, peace on this earth that we live on, peace in all the waters in this universe; may all the herbs, trees and vegetation of this universe experience peace. May the transcendental Lord and each member of His creation be at peace. May your entire lives be saturated with peace.

Om (Aum) - The Lord; *shanti* - may The Lord protect us from all harm emanating from the sky in the form of thunder, lightning and floods etc. (*Adidaivika*).

Om (Aum) - The Lord; *shanti* - may The Lord protect us from all harm emanating from this earth e.g. murderer, theft and injury (*Adhibhautica*).

Om (Aum) - The Lord; *shanti* - May The Lord protect us from all forms of self-harm (*Adhyatmica*).

Benefits of chanting this mantra

- Promotes peace of mind.
- Aids in the development of love, care and concern for the welfare of all members of God's creation.

Reference

Yajur Veda 36:17.

Printed in Great Britain
by Amazon